NEPTUNE

Also by Elaine Landau

ALZHEIMER'S DISEASE

BLACK MARKET ADOPTION AND
THE SALE OF CHILDREN

COWBOYS

JUPITER

LYME DISEASE

MARS

NAZI WAR CRIMINALS

ROBERT FULTON

SATURN

THE SIOUX

SURROGATE MOTHERS

TROPICAL RAIN FORESTS AROUND THE WORLD

WE HAVE AIDS

WILDFLOWERS AROUND THE WORLD

ELAINE LANDAU

NEPTUNE

A FIRST BOOK
FRANKLIN WATTS
NEW YORK/LONDON/TORONTO/SYDNEY/1991

For Bari Braunstein

Cover photograph courtesy of: N.A.S.A.
All photographs courtesy of: N.A.S.A. except: Historical Picture
Service: p. 15 both.

Library of Congress Cataloging-in-Publication Data

Landau, Elaine.
  Neptune / by Elaine Landau.
    p.   cm. — (A First book)
  Includes bibliographical references and index.
  Summary: Uses photographs and other recent findings to describe
the atmosphere and geographic features of Neptune.
  ISBN 0-531-20014-0
  1. Neptune (Planet)—Juvenile literature.   (1. Neptune (Planet))
I. Title. II. Series.
08691.L36   1991
523.4'81—dc20   90-13098 CIP AC

CONTENTS

NEPTUNE

NEPTUNE

CHAPTER ONE

Neptune is a distant and mysterious blue-green planet. It was named after the ancient Roman god of the sea. The god Neptune was thought to rule the oceans and waterways. People believed that he could start or stop sea storms at whim.

Sea travel was extremely important to the ancient Romans. A great deal of their food, cloth, and building materials were imported from other countries. These goods were shipped to their shores, so they were extremely dependent on the sea.

During ancient times, sea travel could be very dangerous. Many sailors didn't survive distant voyages to faraway lands. Roman sailors and their families prayed to Neptune to grant them safe passage.

A color-enhanced photo of the blue-green planet Neptune.

The planet Neptune is one of nine planets that make up our *solar system.* The solar system consists of the sun and the planets, moons, and other objects that revolve around it. Neptune is among the planets furthest away from the sun. In fact, Neptune is so distant, that it is thirty times farther from the sun than Earth.

The planet Neptune is actually quite large. Its diameter is approximately 30,200 miles (48,600 km). That means that Neptune is nearly four times broader than Earth. However, in spite of Neptune's large size, until recently scientists did not know very much about the planet. This is because Neptune is so far away.

There's an interesting story behind Neptune's discovery. Because of its distance from Earth, scientists were unable to clearly see Neptune through their telescopes. They thought it was just another dim star. However, some individuals suspected that this faraway star might be a planet. Their reasoning had to do with the way in which another planet behaved.

Scientists had been observing the planet Uranus for some time. Uranus is Neptune's neighbor, but it is closer to both Earth and the sun. Scientists were fairly certain that Uranus had to be the most faraway planet. Yet at times Uranus behaved un-

This picture shows a background of stars,
the solar system, and galaxy. Neptune is a
distant planet in our solar system.

usually. This led some *astronomers* to question that belief.

For example, it was noted that Uranus was not always positioned where it was expected to be as it revolved around the sun. Was it possible that a yet undiscovered planet, even further out in space, could be affecting Uranus? This would account for the unexpected changes in Uranus's *orbit*, or path.

In 1843 a young British astronomer and mathematician named John C. Adams set out to prove this theory. He was determined to show the existence of a planet that was too far away to be clearly seen from Earth without a telescope. According to Adams's calculations, the new planet would be about a billion miles (1.6 billion km) further from Earth than Uranus.

Although no one realized it at the time, John C. Adams's predictions were amazingly correct. His mathematical conclusions closely pinpointed the then still unknown planet Neptune.

Thinking that he might be on the verge of an important scientific breakthrough, the young scientist sent his findings to a leading authority in the field of astronomy at the time. This was Sir George B. Airy, the Astronomer Royal of England. But unfortunately, Airy did not take Adams's theory about the existence of a new planet seriously. He set aside Adams's claims and chose not to look further into the matter.

At the same time this was going on, a young mathematician from France unknown to John C. Adams had also been working on the same theory. His name was Urbain I. I. Leverrier, and, as it turned out, his research findings proved to be quite similar to those of Adams.

Although the two men had come up with nearly the same answers, Leverrier's research was more favorably received. The Frenchman completed his work by the summer of 1846. At that point, he sent his findings to the Urania Observatory in Berlin, Germany.

The observatory director, Johann G. Galle, investigated Leverrier's data. Galle, along with his assistant, posted the Frenchman's findings on a star chart they'd recently completed. It was an exciting time at the observatory. Galle had received Leverrier's message on September 23, 1846, and found Neptune that very night! With Leverrier's theory confirmed, the planet Neptune was formally acknowledged. Since John C. Adams had reached the same conclusions, today both men are credited with the discovery of this distant planet.

Sir George B. Airy (left) was a highly respected astronomer. However, when he failed to take John Adams's work seriously, Leverrier (right) nearly won sole credit for Neptune's discovery.

Neptune revolves around the sun as do the other planets. However, because Neptune is so far away, it takes this outer planet quite a long time to complete its journey. The Earth needs 365 days, or one year, to revolve around the sun. But Neptune requires approximately 165 years (Earth time) to finish its orbit. In fact, Neptune will not have completed its first trip around the sun since its discovery until the year 2011!

At the same time that Neptune revolves around the sun, it also whirls about in space. This turning or spinning motion is known as *rotation.* Every planet spins, or rotates, as it orbits the sun.

Neptune, as well as the other planets, spins on its rotational *axis.* An axis is an invisible line through a planet's center on which it turns. The Earth spins, or rotates, every twenty-four hours. Neptune rotates once every sixteen hours. That means that a day on Neptune is about sixteen hours long (Earth time).

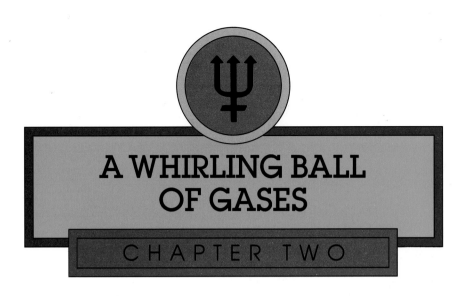

A WHIRLING BALL OF GASES

CHAPTER TWO

Like others of the outer planets in our solar system (Jupiter, Saturn, Uranus), Neptune is largely a gaseous planet. Earth, on the other hand, is considered a solid planet. Neptune's gaseous, fluid makeup makes it extremely different from our planet.

You couldn't stand, jog, or ride a horse on a huge ball of gases and fluids. But there's another reason you couldn't do these things on Neptune. And that's because human beings couldn't survive there.

Neptune lacks the oxygen we need to live. The distant planet's temperatures are also extremely low. Like Earth, Neptune experiences seasons and temperature changes. However, a warm

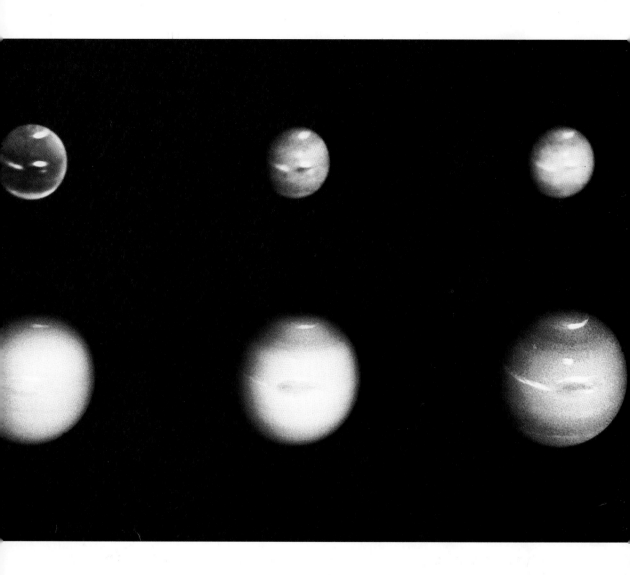

These photos of Neptune taken
through various camera filters show
details of Neptune's atmosphere.

day on Neptune would still be unimaginably cold.

Even with the use of high-powered telescopes, Neptune cannot be seen clearly from Earth. Viewing Neptune from a telescope, the planet looks something like a fuzzy turquoise ball. What we actually may be seeing is a thick top layer of clouds covering the planet. Scientists think that the clouds around Neptune may be made up of ice crystals and methane.

Under the clouds, the *atmosphere* blanketing Neptune may largely consist of hydrogen and helium. Smaller amounts of methane and perhaps ethane may be found as well. Neptune's atmosphere is sizable. Astronomers think that it may be over 2,000 miles (3,200 km) thick.

Within Neptune's interior, the gases comprising the planet may be denser or more tightly packed together. Yet scientists suspect that the only solid portion of Neptune may be a small core of rocky material at the planet's very center.

Neptune appears to have distinct weather patterns. Winds up to 700 miles (1,127 km) per hour sweep across the planet. These winds blow in the opposite direction of the planet's rotation.

Scientists have also noted a dark oval blotch on the planet just below Neptune's *equator* (an

imaginary circle around the planet's center). They suspect that this huge dark mark is actually a turbulent storm center. It's called the Great Dark Spot. The storm center is so large that scientists think it's probably about the size of the planet Earth.

Thin wisps of cirrus clouds appear around the Great Dark Spot. They seem to almost cling to the massive storm center. In photographs, the clouds look somewhat like the hazy morning mist often seen above mountaintops. Cirrus clouds are white feathery clouds that usually appear in tufts or bands. When they were found on Neptune, it was the first time cirrus clouds had ever been spotted on an outer planet.

Neptune's cirrus clouds are actually made of frozen methane gas. These clouds have also been seen racing across regions surrounding Neptune's equator. The clouds cast shadows on Neptune's atmosphere. Their shadows can be seen as far as thirty miles (48 km) below.

A close-up view of
high-altitude cloud streaks
in Neptune's atmosphere

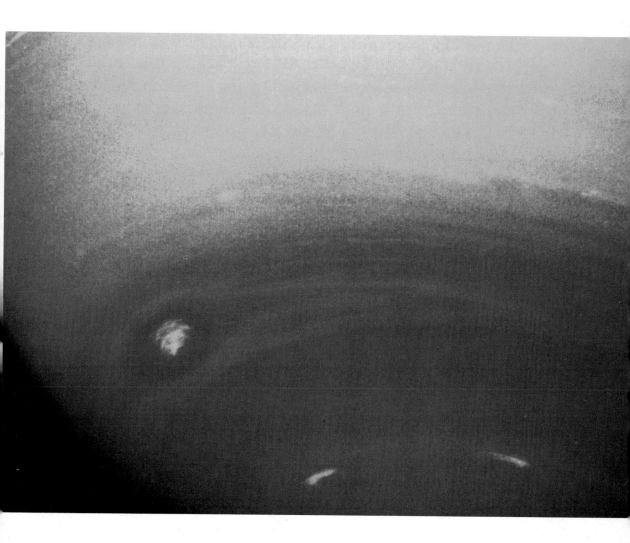

(Facing page) A detailed look at Neptune's
Great Dark Spot. Notice the wispy white
clouds surrounding this stormy area.
(Above) Neptune's cloud systems in
the planet's southern hemisphere.

Astronomers have found other interesting features on Neptune. Just below the Great Dark Spot, a fast-moving cloud appears. Scientists have nicknamed this cloud "Scooter" because of its rapid motion. There's also another smaller but distinct storm system on Neptune. Because it's similar to the Great Dark Spot, scientists have called this storm Dark Spot 2. In addition, numerous cyclonelike storms may be occurring on Neptune.

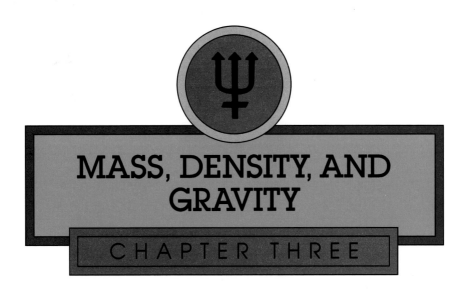

MASS, DENSITY, AND GRAVITY

When describing or comparing the various planets within our solar system, scientists will often refer to a planet's *mass.* A planet's mass represents the total amount of material of which it is composed. Neptune is an extremely large planet. Its mass is nearly seventeen times greater than that of Earth.

Planets are often compared in terms of *density* as well as mass. A planet's density is a measure of how tightly compressed, or packed together, are the materials of which it is made. Solid planets, such as Earth, tend to have a greater density than gaseous or fluid planets. Although Neptune is larger in size, or has a greater mass, than Earth, its density is less than our planet's. This means that a portion of Neptune's matter would weigh less than an equal portion of Earth's matter. Earth has the highest density of any of the nine planets that revolve around the sun.

Gravity is a powerful but invisible force that draws objects toward a planet's center. The effects of gravity are all around us. If you toss a Frisbee in a park and no one catches it, it will fall to the ground. Gravity is the force that pulls it down. During a hail or ice storm, gravity causes these tiny frozen droplets to hit the pavement. Earth's gravity keeps the moon orbiting the planet. Otherwise, it might drift off into space.

Gravitational pull, such as that experienced on Earth, is present on the other planets as well. Neptune's gravity keeps the planet's moons orbiting it, just as Earth's gravity holds our moon captive.

SPACE PROBES

In August 1989, the *Voyager 2* spacecraft flew past Neptune. Its view of the planet completed a grand tour of four planets that spanned a twelve-year journey through space.

In 1979 *Voyager 2*'s first encounter was with the planet Jupiter. From there it went on to Saturn in 1981 and later Uranus in 1986. Finally in 1989 it reached Neptune—the distant planet about which relatively little was known.

The one-ton space *probe* actually came quite close to the planet. As it approached Neptune, *Voyager 2* picked up speed, so that it was traveling at a rate of 60,980 miles (98,135 km) per hour. The space probe swooped down to an area about 3,000 miles (4,830 km) above Neptune's frozen methane clouds.

A painting of the *Voyager 2* spacecraft
as it looks back upon Neptune
and its moon Triton.

Then, as it had been programmed to do, the space probe made a sharp turn. At that point it headed for Neptune's wondrous frosty pink-and-white moon—Triton. *Voyager 2* was able to pass within 24,000 miles (38,623 km) of Triton's colorful, rocky exterior.

Signals from the space probe's television cameras and technical instruments were carried back to Earth by radio waves. Radio waves travel at the speed of light (186,282 miles (299,792 km) per second). Information about Neptune transmitted by *Voyager 2* arrived on Earth four hours and six minutes later.

From there it was decoded at the Jet Propulsion Laboratory in Pasadena, California. Within minutes, the *Voyager 2* data appeared on the lab's viewing screens and computer stations. It was an exciting time for both the scientists working on the project and the millions of Americans who watched the thrilling space drama unfold live on their television screens at home. As one astronomer at the Jet Propulsion Laboratory said of *Voyager 2*'s Neptune fly-by—"This is it! We are exploring new worlds! (Neptune) is not a gee-whiz, science fiction, special effects movie. It's a real place."

Following its view of Triton, the spacecraft

These television cameras aboard
Voyager 2 provided photographs of
Neptune's atmosphere and unusual features.

This photo taken by *Voyager 2* shows Neptune's moon Triton and a portion of Neptune.

A view of Neptune's south pole as *Voyager 2* flew by the blue-green planet.

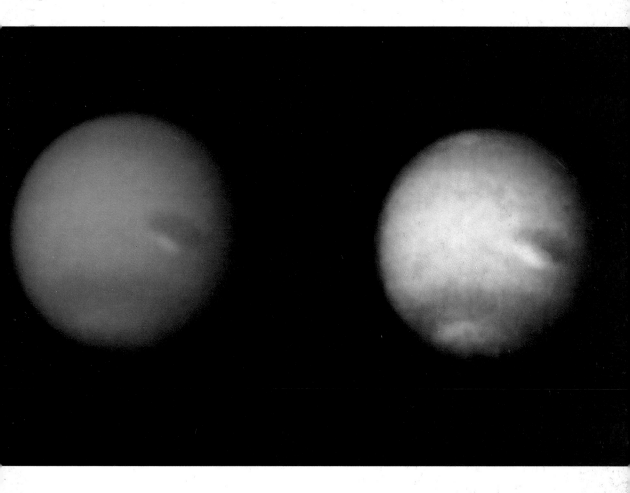

More color pictures obtained by *Voyager 2*.
The photo on the left shows Neptune as it
would appear to the human eye. The right-
hand photo was enhanced to highlight
details. Notice the darkish ring, or collar,
around the planet's south pole.

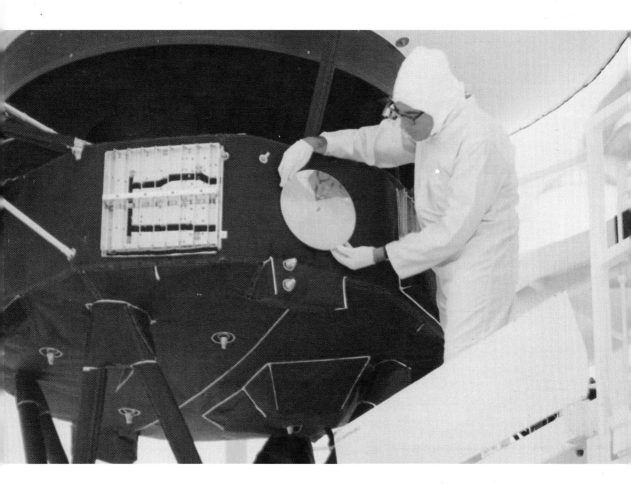

The *Sounds of Earth* record containing earthly
music and language is mounted on the *Voyager 2*
spacecraft at the Kennedy Space Center
in Florida. The gold-plated copper record was
encased in a gold-plated shield to protect it
during the spacecraft's flight past Neptune to
the outer edges of the solar system.

headed out to the distant fringes of the solar system. Scientists hope that *Voyager 2* will continue to send back information for at least the next twenty-five years. If all goes well, the spacecraft may send back data until the year 2020.

Throughout *Voyager 2's* vast journey, it had sent back images to Earth that had never been seen before. Its view of Neptune and its moons yielded volumes of new information. It will take scientists years to study, test, and fully understand all that can be learned from the *Voyager 2* visits.

Yet even at this time, many scientists believe they already know more about Neptune from *Voyager 2's* findings than has been learned since the planet's discovery in 1846. Although astronomers are enthusiastic about new incoming data, they feel that the spacecraft's journey has already been an overwhelming success. As Edward Stone, the Voyager mission's chief scientist, said, "This has been the journey of a lifetime."

NEPTUNE'S RINGS

CHAPTER FIVE

Scientists working on data collected by *Voyager 2* think that a total of five rings may surround Neptune. They aren't sure of the exact number. It's possible that the three rings between the planet's outermost ring and the ring closest to Neptune might instead be a single ring. Astronomers are still working on this puzzling question.

Neptune's rings are not solid bodies. Rather, they are composed of tiny frozen bits of matter that follow nearly the same orbit around the planet. Neptune's outermost ring (the one farthest away from the planet) is quite bright. It also has some unusual features.

Scientists discovered six to eight icy objects within the ring itself. These objects tend to be

Neptune's rings as photographed
by *Voyager 2*

somewhat small in size. The largest is no bigger than between 6 to 12 miles (10 to 19 km) wide.

Scientists call these icy objects moonlets. The objects give the bright ring a somewhat clumpy appearance. This is because they make parts of the ring wider or bulkier than the other sections of the circle.

NEPTUNE'S MOONS

CHAPTER SIX

For many years Neptune was thought to have only two moons, or satellites, orbiting it. These moons, named Triton and Nereid, had been discovered from Earth. Scientists had located them with high-powered telescopic equipment. *Voyager 2*'s findings greatly expanded our knowledge about Neptune's moons, though. Today we know that Neptune has not two but at least eight moons.

The moon called Triton is especially fascinating. Triton is Neptune's largest moon. In photographs taken by *Voyager 2*, it appears as a frosty pink-and-white ball. It is also streaked with blue blotches.

Scientists think that Triton may be the coldest

Voyager 2 discovered new moons orbiting Neptune. Among them is the moon called Satellite 1989 pictured here.

place in the solar system. Temperatures near the moon's surface may be as low as 400 degrees Fahrenheit (240° Celsius) below zero. When we see the moon's pink-and-white outer color, we may actually be looking at a layer of methane, nitrogen, and carbon dioxide that has frozen solid in the extreme cold.

Photographs of Triton taken by *Voyager 2* show the moon as a spectacular world of ice. Much of its surface looks like a fairy-tale winter wonderland. Along with steep mountains and rugged cliffs, it has many faults (fractures or breaks in the ice formation). Triton also has some craters.

Among the most wondrous findings of *Voyager 2* was the discovery of ice volcanoes on the pinkish moon. This was the first time astronomers had actually ever seen an ice volcano.

Triton's ice volcanoes spew nitrogen ice and gas to a height of about twenty-five miles (40 km). The ice and gas are shot out at tremendous speeds approaching 560 miles (901 km) per hour. Geologists suspect that these ice volcanoes are either active on Triton today or have been active within the past three hundred years.

Voyager 2 also photographed immense *calderas* on Triton. A caldera is a crater left by a vol-

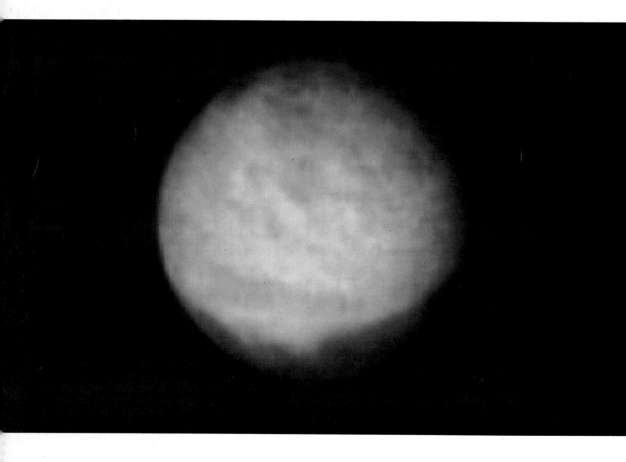

(Above) Neptune's moon Triton as photographed by *Voyager 2*. Triton's overall pinkish
color may be due to reddish materials
produced by its methane gas and ice.
(Right) This is a false-color photo combination
of Triton. The white areas may be ice.
The dark material alongside the long, narrow
canyons appears to be volcanic deposits.

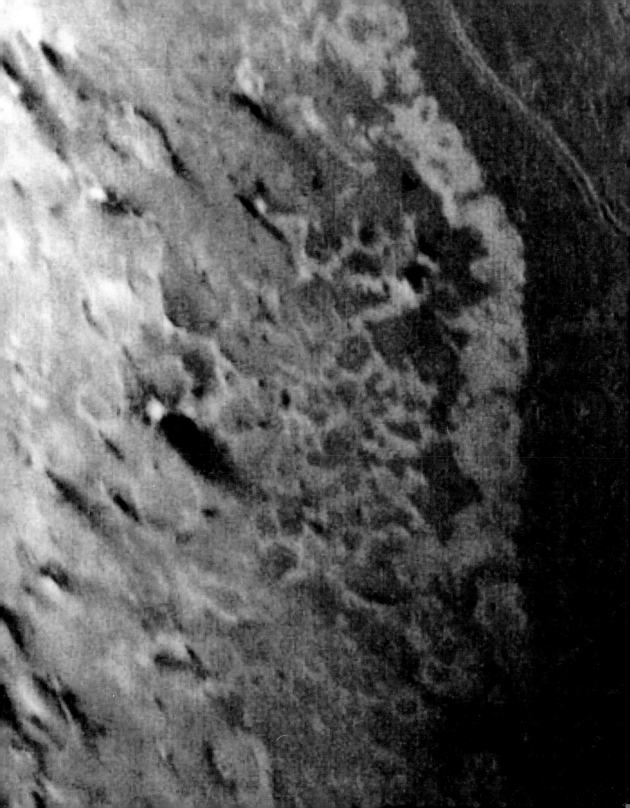

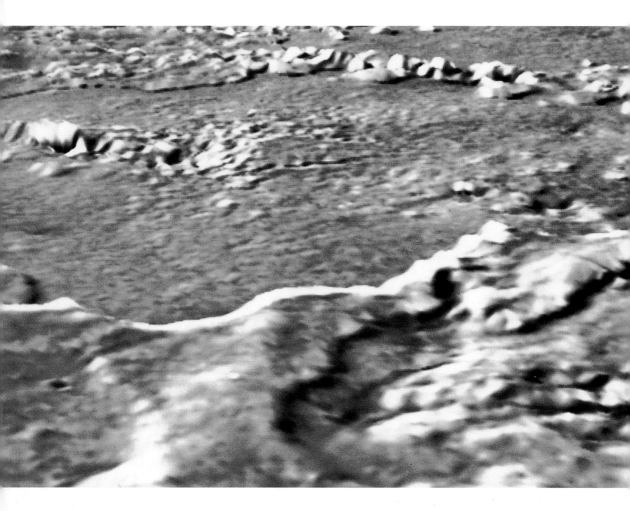

A computer-created view of one of
Triton's caldera-like depressions.
(Facing page) A look at Triton from a distance
of 25,000 miles (40,250 km). The depressions
shown here may be caused by the melting and
collapsing of the moon's icy surface.

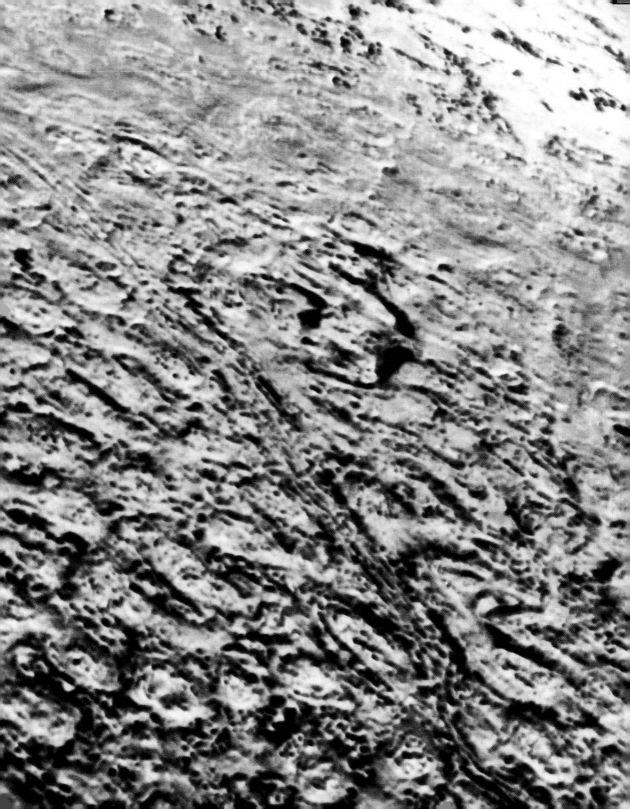

canic eruption. These craters may be over 1,000 feet (305 m) deep and can measure hundreds of miles (or kilometers) across.

One astronomer from the Jet Propulsion Laboratory described the ice volcanoes as something we might expect to see in a space horror film. He said that areas of Triton looked like "erupted plastic masses." He went on to describe the moon as being "almost too bizarre to be believed." *Voyager 2* may have provided us with pictures of the greatest ice show in outer space.

THE FUTURE

CHAPTER SEVEN

It may be difficult for us to imagine an icy world such as Triton or even a storm center the size of Earth on Neptune. Yet we know now that such things exist within our solar system.

At this time, no one knows the importance these discoveries may hold for our future.

Bruce Murray, former director of the Jet Propulsion Laboratory, told the press, "The discoveries challenge our imagination and seem like science fiction. But they may be very important to our grandchildren and their grandchildren." Vice-president Dan Quayle echoed these feelings when he stated, "We Americans have been opening new frontiers throughout our history and we will continue to do so. Today, space is America's frontier."

A colorful collage featuring the space program's
many achievements. Some researchers
believe our greatest challenges lie ahead.

FACT SHEET ON NEPTUNE

Symbol for Neptune— ♆

Position—In average distance, Neptune is the eighth planet from the sun (Earth is the third). It's usually positioned between the planets Uranus and Pluto.

Rotation period—approximately 16 hours

Length of year—approximately 165 years (Earth time)

Diameter—30,200 miles (48,600 km)

Distance from the sun (depending on location in orbit)—least: 2,754,000,000 miles (4,432,500,000 km); greatest: 2,832,000,000 miles (4,539,800,000 km)

Distance from the Earth (depending on orbit)—least: 2,700,000,000 miles (4,350,000,000 km); greatest: 2,750,000,000 miles (4,426,000,000 km)

Number of moons—Neptune has at least eight moons. The largest of these are Triton and a newly discovered moon temporarily named "1989 Ni." 1989 Ni is larger than Neptune's other long-known moon, Nereid.

GLOSSARY

Astronomers—scientists who study the planets, stars, and all of outer space

Atmosphere—the combination of various gases that covers some bodies in space

Axis—the invisible line through a planet's center around which it spins, or rotates

Caldera—the hole or crater created by a volcanic eruption

Crater—a hole on a planet, moon, or other solid body formed by a collision with an object in space

Density—the compactness of the materials that make up a planet

Equator—an imaginary circle around a planet midway between its poles, which divides it into two separate parts called hemispheres

Gravity—the force that pulls objects toward the center of a planet

Mass—the amount of matter; the body or bulk of a planet

Orbit—the curved path followed by a body revolving around another body in space

Probe—spacecraft carrying scientific instruments that orbits the sun on its way to one or more planets; in doing so, it may fly past a planet it has been aimed at, orbit the planet, or, in some cases, even land there. Planetary probes collect a great deal of data about a planet even from distances of millions or billions of miles

Rotation—the process by which a planet spins, or turns, on its axis as it orbits the sun

Satellite—a body that revolves around a planet, such as a moon; or, a manufactured device launched from Earth into orbit

Solar system—the sun and all the objects that travel around it; such objects include planets, moons, chunks of iron and stone called meteorites, asteroids, and even tiny flakes of dust

FOR FURTHER READING

Apfel, Necia H. *Nebulae: The Birth and Death of Stars.* New York: Lothrop, 1988.

Branley, Franklyn M. *Eclipse: Darkness in the Daytime.* New York: Crowell, 1988.

Furniss, Tim. *Our Future in Space.* New York: Franklin Watts, 1986.

Jay, Michael. *Planets.* New York: Franklin Watts, 1987.

Lauber, Patricia. *Journey to the Planets.* New York: Crown, 1982.

Simon, Seymour. *Jupiter.* New York: Morrow, 1985.

Wyler, Rose. *Starry Night.* Englewood Cliffs, New Jersey: Prentice Hall, 1989.

INDEX